A Non-engineers approach to
Battery Technology

Poovaiah Malavanda & Sanjan P S

A Non-engineers approach to Battery Technology

A handbook on Battery Technology for Non-engineers

© 2018 Poovaiah Malavanda & Sanjan P S

Cover, Illustrations: Cariappa K P

Editing: Poovaiah Malavanda

Other contributors: Nuthan P

Publisher: Amazon KDP

ISBN

Paperback   9781980516606

Contents

Table of Contents

About the authors

Poovaiah Malavanda

Poovaiah was born on the 11th of April, 1998 in the South of Kodagu, India. He is from a humble middle-class family whose family occupation is Coffee Plantation, way back from childhood Poovaiah was a Science & Technology enthusiast and has worked on numerous IOT projects and hobby projects.

Poovaiah is an Engineering dropout and is pursuing his carrier in Management field.

In 2016 Poovaiah joined a startup called Dvizira Pvt Ltd, a company started by few like-minded people. Joining the company as an intern then Poovaiah worked under the mentorship of Mr.Nuthan P, CEO of Dvizira Pvt Ltd & the CTO of Bellatrix Aerospace, during this period Poovaiah gained a depth of knowledge on Systems Engineering and Project Management.

Currently, Poovaiah works as a Project Manager in Dvizira Pvt Ltd. Poovaiah leads a team which is currently working on projects of health and defense sector.

A big believer in hard work and dedication supports Entrepreneurship and skill development.

Poovaiah is no stranger to technology having spent about three years working on Battery Technology. Prior to work in the management field, Poovaiah had spent few years working on a project called "Active Battery Management System" and also wrote a research paper on "Active charge balancing in Li-ion battery" along with the co-author of this book Mr.Sanjan PS and a mutual friend.

Poovaiah is also passionate about Military and is currently working on projects to aid the soldier's hard lifestyle and to support them during combat.

Sanjan PS

Sanjan is an electronic hobbyist and likes to savage and build things. He started off with electronics when he was 10 years old, the knowledge of which he gained by reading books and the internet.

"The best way to learn how something works is by breaking it apart, straining your head about it and analyzing how it works is the key to getting new ideas or improving something that already exists," he says. Basically, the kind of person who went "3D printing services are expensive, so I will build a 3D printer itself" kind of a person.

Sanjan wants to help the society and works for NGO's. Currently pursuing his Bachelor's Degree in Electrical Engineering in Mysore, He is interested in renewable energy, power management, smart grids, and microgrids. His goal is to provide self-sustained power supply to people who still don't have access to electricity. Along with Poovaiah and his classmate, he has developed a new conceptual BMS with the research paper titled "Active charge balancing in Li-Ion cells". Now he is working on it to take it a step further by developing an algorithm and the hardware.

In 2016 Sanjan joined a start-up company called Dvizira Pvt Ltd as a research intern. Now he is working as a full-time employee for it.

9

GLOSSARY: Glossary of Technical Battery Terminology

Accumulator - A rechargeable battery or cell.

Ampere or Amp - An Ampere or an Amp is a unit of measurement for an electrical current. One amp is the amount of current produced by an electromotive force of one volt acting through the resistance of one ohm. Named for the French physicist Andre Marie Ampere. The abbreviation for Amp is A but its mathematical symbol is "I". Small currents are measured in milli-Amps or thousandths of an Amp.

Amp Hour or Ampere-Hour - A unit of measurement of a battery's electrical storage capacity. Current multiplied by time in hours equals ampere-hours. One amp hour is equal to a current of one ampere flowing for one hour. Also, 1 amp hour is equal to 1,000 mAh

Ampere-Hour Capacity - The number of ampere-hours which can be delivered by a battery on a single discharge.

Anode - During discharge, the negative electrode of the cell is the anode whereas in charge, that reverses and the positive electrode of the cell is the anode. The anode gives up electrons to the load circuit and dissolves into the electrolyte.

Aqueous Batteries - Batteries with water-based electrolytes. The electrolyte may not appear to be liquid since it can be absorbed by the battery's separator.

Actual Capacity or Available Capacity - The total battery capacity, usually expressed in ampere-hours or milliampere-hours, available to perform work. The actual capacity of a particular battery is determined by a number of factors, including the cut-off voltage, discharge rate, temperature, method of charge and the age and life history of the battery.

Battery - An electrochemical device used to store energy. The term is usually applied to a group of two or more electric cells connected together electrically. In common usage, the term "battery" is also applied to a single cell, such as an AA battery.

Battery Capacity - The electric output of a cell or battery on a service test delivered before the cell reaches a specified final electrical condition and may be expressed in ampere-hours, watt-hours, or similar units. The capacity in watt-hours is equal to the capacity in ampere-hours multiplied by the battery voltage.

Battery Charger - A device capable of supplying electrical energy to a battery.

Battery-Charge Rate - The current expressed in amperes (A) or milliamps (mA) at which a battery is charged.

Cutoff Voltage, final - The prescribed lower-limit voltage at which battery discharge is considered complete. The cutoff or final voltage is usually chosen so that the maximum useful capacity of the battery is realized. The cutoff voltage varies with the type of battery and the kind of service in which the battery is used. When testing the capacity of a NiMH or NiCD battery a cutoff voltage of 1.0 V is normally used. 0.9V is normally used as the cutoff voltage of an alkaline cell. A device that is designed with too high a cutoff voltage may stop operating while the battery still has significant capacity remaining.

12

C - Used to signify a charge or discharge rate equal to the capacity of a battery divided by 1 hour. Thus C for a 1600 mAh battery would be 1.6 A, C/5 for the same battery would be 320 mA and C/10 would be 160 mA. Because C is dependent on the capacity of a battery the C rate for batteries of different capacities must also be different.

Capacity - The capacity of a battery is a measure of the amount of energy that it can deliver in a single discharge. Battery capacity is normally listed as amp-hours (or milliamp-hours) or as watt-hours.

Cathode - Is an electrode that, in effect, oxidizes the anode or absorbs the electrons. During discharge, the positive electrode of a voltaic cell is the cathode. When charging, that reverses and the negative electrode of the cell is the cathode.

Cell - An electrochemical device, composed of positive and negative plates and electrolyte, which is capable of storing electrical energy. It is the basic "building block" of a battery.

Charge - The conversion of electric energy, provided in the form of a current, into chemical energy within the cell or battery.

Charge Rate - The amount of current applied to the battery during the charging process. This rate is commonly expressed as a fraction of the capacity of the battery. For example, the C/2 or C/5.

Charging - The process of supplying electrical energy for conversion to stored chemical energy.

Constant-Current Charge - A charging process in which the current applied to the battery is maintained at a constant value.

Constant-Voltage Charge - A charging process in which the voltage applied to a battery is held at a constant value.

Cycle - One sequence of charge and discharge.

Deep Cycle - A cycle in which the discharge is continued until the battery reaches its cut-off voltage, usually 80% of discharge.

Shallow Cycling - Charge and discharge cycles which do not allow the battery to approach its cutoff voltage. Shallow cycling of NiCd cells leads to "memory effect". Shallow cycling is not detrimental to NiMH cells and it is the most beneficial for lead-acid batteries.

Cycle Life - For rechargeable batteries, the total number of charge/discharge cycles the cell can sustain before its capacity is significantly reduced. End of life is usually considered to be reached when the cell or battery delivers only 80% of rated ampere-hour capacity. NiMH batteries typically have a cycle life of 500 cycles, NiCd batteries can have a cycle life of over 1,000 cycles. The cycle of a battery is greatly influenced by the type depth of the cycle (deep or shallow) and the method of recharging. Improper charge cycle cutoff can greatly reduce the cycle life of a battery.

Direct Current (DC) - The type of electrical current that a battery can supply. One terminal is always positive and another is always negative.

Discharge - The conversion of the chemical energy of the battery into electric energy.

The Depth of Discharge - The amount of energy that has been removed from a battery (or battery pack). Usually expressed as a percentage of the total capacity of the battery. For example, 50%

depth of discharge means that half of the energy in the battery has been used. 80% DOD means that eighty percent of the energy has been discharged, so the battery now holds only 20% of its full charge.

Discharge, deep - Withdrawal of all electrical energy to the end-point voltage before the cell or battery is recharged.

Discharge, high-rate - Withdrawal of large currents for short intervals of time, usually at a rate that would completely discharge a cell or battery in less than one hour.

Discharge, low-rate - Withdrawal of small currents for long periods of time, usually longer than one hour.

Drain - Withdrawal of current from a cell.

Dry Cell - A primary cell in which the electrolyte is absorbed in a porous medium, or is otherwise restrained from flowing. Common practice limits the term "dry cell" to the Leclanch, cell, which is the common commercial type.

Electrochemical Couple - The system of active materials within a cell that provides electrical energy storage through an electrochemical reaction.

Electrode - An electrical conductor through which an electric current enters or leaves a conducting medium, whether it be an electrolytic solution, solid, molten mass, gas, or vacuum. For electrolytic solutions, many solids, and molten masses, an electrode is an electrical conductor at the surface of which a change occurs from conduction by electrons to conduction by ions. For gases and vacuum, the electrodes merely serve to conduct electricity to and from the medium.

Electrolyte - A chemical compound which, when fused or dissolved in certain solvents, usually water, will conduct an electric current. All electrolytes in the fused state or in solution give rise to ions which conduct the electric current.

Electropositivity - The degree to which an element in a galvanic cell will function as the positive elements of the cell. An element with a large electro positivity will oxidize faster than an element with a smaller electropositivity.

End-of-Discharge Voltage - The voltage of the battery at the termination of a discharge.

Energy - Output Capability - expressed as capacity time's voltage or watt-hours.

Energy Density - Ratio of cell energy to weight or volume (watt-hours per pound, or watt-hours per cubic inch).

Final Voltage (see Cutoff voltage)

Float Charging - Method of recharging in which a secondary cell is continuously connected to a constant-voltage supply that maintains the cell in fully charged condition. Typically applied to lead-acid batteries.

Galvanic Cell - A combination of electrodes, separated by an electrolyte, that is capable of producing electrical energy by electrochemical action.

Gassing - The evolution of gas from one or both of the electrodes in a cell. Gassing commonly results from self-discharge or from the electrolysis of water in the electrolyte during charging.

Internal Resistance - The resistance to the flow of an electric current within the cell or battery.

Memory Effect - A phenomenon in which a cell, operated in successive cycles to less than full, depth of discharge, temporarily loses the remainder of its capacity at normal voltage levels (usually applies only to Ni-Cd cells). Note, memory effect can be induced in NiCd cells even if the level of discharge is not the same during each cycle. Memory effect is reversible.

Negative Terminal - The terminal of a battery from which electrons flow in the external circuit when the cell discharges. See Positive Terminal.

Nonaqueous Batteries - Cells that do not contain water, such as those with molten salts or organic electrolytes.

Ohm's Law - The formula that describes the amount of current flowing through a circuit. Ohm's Law - In a given electrical circuit, the amount of current in amperes (I) is equal to the pressure in volts (V) divided by the resistance, in ohms (R). Ohm's law can be shown by three different formulas:

To find Current WE= V/R

To find Voltage V = WEx R

To find Resistance R = V/I

Open Circuit - Condition of a battery which is neither in charge nor on discharge (i.e., disconnected from a circuit).

Open-Circuit Voltage - The difference in potential between the terminals of a cell when the circuit is open (i.e., a no-load condition).

Oxidation - A chemical reaction that results in the release of electrons by an electrode's active material.

Parallel Connection - The arrangement of cells in a battery made by connecting all positive terminals together and all negative terminals together. The voltage of the group remains the same as the voltage of the individual cell. The capacity is increased in proportion to the number of cells.

Polarity - Refers to the charges residing at the terminals of a battery.

Positive Terminal - The terminal of a battery toward which electrons flow through the external circuit when the cell discharges. See Negative Terminal.

Primary Battery - A battery made up of primary cells. See Primary Cell.

Primary Cell - A cell designed to produce electric current through an electrochemical reaction that is not efficiently reversible. The cell, when discharged, cannot be efficiently recharged by an electric current. Alkaline, lithium, and zinc air are common types of primary cells.

Rated Capacity - The number of ampere-hours a cell can deliver under specific conditions (rate of discharge, end voltage, temperature); usually the manufacturer's rating.

Rechargeable - Capable of being recharged; refers to secondary cells or batteries.

Recombination - State in which the gases normally formed within the battery cell during its operation are recombined to form water.

Reduction - A chemical process that results in the acceptance of electrons by an electrode's active material.

Seal - The structural part of a galvanic cell that restricts the escape of solvent or electrolyte from the cell and limits the ingress of air into the cell (the air may dry out the electrolyte or interfere with the chemical reactions).

Secondary Battery - A battery made up of secondary cells. See Storage Battery; Storage Cell.

Self Discharge - Discharge that takes place while the battery is in an open-circuit condition.

Separator - The permeable membrane that allows the passage of ions, but prevents electrical contact between the anode and the cathode.

Series Connection - The arrangement of cells in a battery configured by connecting the positive terminal of each successive cell to the negative terminal of the next adjacent cell so that their voltages are cumulative. See Parallel Connection.

Shelf Life - For a dry cell, the period of time (measured from the date of manufacture), at a storage temperature of 21 degrees C (69 degrees F), after which the cell retains a specified percentage (usually 90%) of its original energy content.

Short-Circuit - A condition that occurs when a short electrical path is unintentionally created. Batteries can supply hundreds of amps if short-circuited, potentially melting the terminals and creating sparks.

Short-Circuit Current - That current delivered when a cell is short-circuited (i.e., the positive and negative terminals are directly connected with a low-resistance conductor).

Starting-Lighting-Ignition (SLI) Battery - A battery designed to start internal combustion engines and to power the electrical systems in automobiles when the engine is not running. SLWEbatteries can be used in emergency lighting situations.

Stationary Battery - A secondary battery designed for use in a fixed location.

Storage Battery - An assembly of identical cells in which the electrochemical action is reversible so that the battery may be recharged by passing a current through the cells in the opposite direction to that of discharge. While many non-storage batteries have a reversible process, only those that are economically rechargeable are classified as storage batteries. Synonym: Accumulator; Secondary Battery. See Secondary Cell.

Storage Cell - An electrolytic cell for the generation of electric energy in which the cell after being discharged may be restored to a charged condition by an electric current flowing in a direction opposite the flow of current when the cell discharges. Synonym: Secondary Cell. See Storage Battery.

Taper Charge - A charging regime delivering moderately high-rate charging current when the battery is at a low state of charge and tapering the current to lower rates as the battery becomes more fully charged.

Terminals - The parts of a battery to which the external electric circuit is connected.

Thermal Runaway - A condition whereby a cell on charge or discharge will destroy itself through internal heat generation caused by high overcharge or high rate of discharge or other abusive conditions.

Trickle Charging - A method of recharging in which a secondary cell is either continuously or intermittently connected to a constant-current supply that maintains the cell in fully charged condition.

Vent - A normally sealed mechanism that allows for the controlled escape of gases from within a cell.

Volt - The unit of measurement of electromotive force, or difference of potential, which will cause a current of one ampere to flow through a resistance of one ohm. Named for Italian physicist Alessandro Volta (1745-1827).

Voltage, cutoff - Voltage at the end of useful discharge. (See Voltage, end-point.)

Voltage, end-point - Cell voltage below which the connected equipment will not operate or below which operation is not recommended.

Voltage, nominal - Voltage of a fully charged cell when delivering rated current.

Watt - A measurement of total power. It is amperes multiplied by volts. 120 volt @ 1 amp = 12 volts @ 10 amps.

Wet Cell - A cell, the electrolyte of which is in liquid form and free to flow and move.

Chapter 1: The development and the history of Battery

Batteries are so ubiquitous today that they're almost invisible to us. Yet they are a remarkable invention with a long and storied history and an equally exciting future.

A battery is essentially a device that stores chemical energy that is converted into electricity. Basically, batteries are small chemical reactors, with the reaction producing energetic electrons, ready to flow through the external device.

American scientist and inventor Benjamin Franklin first used the term "battery" in 1749   when he was doing experiments with electricity using a set of linked capacitors.

The first true battery was invented by the Italian physicist Alessandro Volta in 1800. Volta stacked discs of copper (Cu) and zinc (Zn) separated by a cloth soaked in salt water.

One of the most enduring batteries, the lead-acid battery, was invented in 1859 and is still the technology used to start most internal combustion engine cars today. It is the oldest example of the rechargeable battery.

Today batteries come in a range of sizes from large Megawatt sizes, which store the power from solar farms or substations to guarantee stable supply in entire villages or islands, down to tiny batteries like those used in electronic watches.

There is now much anticipation that battery technology is about to take another leap with new models being developed with enough capacity to store the power generated with domestic solar or wind systems and then power a home at the convenient time for a few days

Chapter 2: Application of Battery and Market

2.1 Application

Batteries are used in portable consumer instruments like Calculators, iPods, Digital Diaries, Wrist Watches, Stop Watches, Artificial Pacemakers etc.

Lithium Cells can also be used as a replacement for Alkaline Batteries in many devices such as Camera's, Clocks, etc. Although they are more expensive Lithium Batteries will provide much longer life.

From Alkaline to Silver-Dioxide batteries, the different types of batteries are used in the different application. Here are a few different types of Batteries with their application.

- **Zinc-Carbon Batteries**

Zinc-Carbon batteries are also known as dry cells (as the nature of electrolyte used in these cells is dry), which come in a composition of a carbon rod (cathode) surrounded by a mixture of carbon powder and manganese dioxide (to increase the conductivity). This whole combination is packed in a zinc container acting as the anode. The electrolyte is a mixture of ammonium chloride and zinc chloride. The typical voltage value is a little less than 1.5V. These batteries are durable and have longer lives.

These general purpose batteries are available for lower prices which is why many electronic devices are sold with these batteries included free. The basic use is in low power drain applications such as flashlights, remote controls, toys, and table clocks.

• Alkaline Batteries

Alkaline batteries are non-rechargeable, high energy density, batteries that have a long lifespan. This battery obtained its name because the electrolyte used in it is alkaline (potassium hydroxide). The chemical composition features zinc powder as an anode and manganese dioxide as the cathode with potassium hydroxide as the electrolyte.

Alkaline batteries are the most common type of batteries used in the world with major consumption in the US, UK, and Switzerland. Designed for long-lasting performance, these can be found in remote controls, clocks, and radios. The high runtime makes alkaline batteries ideal for digital cameras, handheld games, MP3 players etc.

• Lead-Acid Batteries

Lead-acid batteries are the rechargeable kind of batteries invented in the 1980s. These large, heavyweight batteries find the major application in automobiles as these fulfill the high current requirements of the heavy motors. The composition of Lead-Acid battery changes in charged and discharged states.

The major application of lead acid battery is in starting, lighting, and ignition systems (SLI) of automobiles. Its other form, wet cell battery is used as backup power supply for high-end servers, personal computers, telephone exchanges, and in off-grid homes with inverters. Portable emergency lights also use lead-acid batteries.

- **Mercury Batteries**

Mercury batteries are non-rechargeable batteries that contain mercuric oxide with manganese dioxide. They are deep discharge batteries and voltage level does not fall below 1.35V until 5% energy level is reached. These batteries are less popular because of the low output voltage.

The flat discharge curve makes this battery useful for photographic light meters and electronic devices such as to run the real-time clock of the CPU.

- **Silver Oxide Battery**

These batteries are commonly called as Button Batteries as they are mostly produced in very small sizes. These batteries are not very expensive, hence is very popular in the retail market it's used in small electronic devices like watches and calculators. Large sized Silver-Oxide batteries are made for some customized designs or in the military, where the cost is not the factor. These batteries can be operated even under the heavy draining condition and also at lower temperatures.

The military and the space programme use Silver-Oxide Battery because of the high performance they exhibit. The high energy density characteristics of the Silver-Oxide batteries are used in Military and aerospace industries. They also have the ability to tolerate high current load.

- **Lithium-Ion Battery**

Lithium-Ion batteries are common in home electronics. They are one of the most popular types of rechargeable batteries for portable electronics with high energy density, tiny memory effect and also self-discharge. Lithium-Ion batteries are also growing in popularity for Military, Battery Electric Vehicle & Aerospace application. These batteries have a long list of real-world application beyond running our apps on the phone, from life-saving medical equipment to luxury Yacht, these batteries keep both the essential and comfort of modern life running with safety and reliability.

Most common application of these batteries are in Uninterrupted Power supply system, Dependable Electric and recreational Vehicle Power, Lightweight Marine Vehicles, Solar Power Storage, Surveillance or Alarm systems in remote locations, a Portable power pack that eliminates downtime etc.

We will discuss more on this type of Battery in Chapter 10.

2.2 Market

2.2.1 Industrial Market

The global battery market size was USD 62.00 billion in 2017 on account of high demand from the automotive application. The automotive application includes rechargeable batteries used in electric vehicles and non-rechargeable batteries. Rising popularity of consumer electronics on a global level is expected to result in high lithium-ion batteries over the forecast period. High demand for portable electronics including smartphones, LCD displays, tablets and wearable devices such as fitness bands propel battery market growth. The market is expected to witness significant growth on account of technological advancements in terms of product innovation, enhanced efficiency, and cost-effectiveness.

In 2015, electric vehicle batteries from Tesla and Nissan saw a price cut reaching USD 300 per KWH, hinting a cost parity with conventional vehicles. Stringent emission norms by governments of developed nations including the U.S. and the UK coupled with rising focus towards fuel efficiency is expected to propel market demand. Depleting fossil fuel reserves along with high CO2 emissions and favorable government initiatives are expected to drive battery market in the next eight years. Primary non-rechargeable batteries are widely used in light beacons, children's toys, remote controls, electronic keys, and watches. These are expected to witness a loss of share to rechargeable secondary batteries on account of enhanced lifespan and efficiency of the later. Emerging markets of Asia Pacific and Africa are expected to propel battery demand in electric bicycles and storage applications. Storage applications include load leveling in renewable energy sources including solar and the wind. Increasing automobile and aircraft production in emerging economies of Asia Pacific including India and China is expected to provide immense potential for market growth.

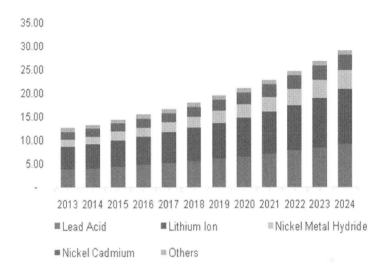

Figure: Global Battery usage Market Share by-region

2.2.2 Product Market

Lead acid battery accounts for a significant share of over 50% in 2015 on account of rising application in automotive, UPS, telecommunication, electric bikes, and transport vehicles. High use of UPS devices in healthcare, chemical and oil & gas sector for continuous power supply will propel lead-acid market demand. These batteries are used in critical applications on account of high reliability and low cost. However, lithium-ion batteries are expected to capture a significant portion of the lead acid battery over the forecast period on account of low energy density and high lead content.

Lithium-ion batteries are expected to penetrate lead-acid battery applications including electric vehicles, plug-in electric vehicles, storage, and automobiles thus, gaining a majority market share by 2024.

Automotive was the largest application on account of rising demand from electric vehicles, hybrid vehicles, and plug-in hybrid vehicles. SLWE application in the automotive sector has contributed to high battery demand for starting, lighting, and ignition of the vehicle. Industrial applications include forklifts and other material handling equipment; telecom, UPS, energy storage, emergency lighting, security, road signs, control & switchgear and medical. Rising population of the above-mentioned applications will directly result in high battery demand over the forecast period. Portable applications include high demand consumer electronics which are expected to result in significantly driving the market. This segment is projected to witness significant growth in terms of shipments, however, with small size and low revenues, it does not contribute to a major portion of the market.

2.2.3 Regional Market

The Asia Pacific is a major consumer of batteries on account of rising automobile production coupled with rapid industrialization generating high demand. China and India are key manufacturing countries in the consumer electronics segment owing to the availability of skilled labor and low production and setup costs. North America and Europe are expected to witness significant growth on account of rising electric vehicle production. Nissan Leaf and Chevrolet Volt accounted for over 50% percent of the electric vehicles sold in the U.S. in 2014.

Ford Fusion and C-Max Energy along with Toyota Prius are leading plug-in hybrid electric vehicles in the U.S. Electric Vehicle

Initiative encourages the adoption of electric vehicles on a global scale. It was launched in 2010 under the Clean Energy Ministerial with participating countries including UK, France, Spain, Portugal, U.S. South Africa, Denmark, Netherlands, Sweden, Finland, Germany, Italy, China, India, and Japan.

Chapter 3: Principle of operation

The basis for a battery operation is the exchange of electrons between two chemical reactions, an oxidation reaction, and a reduction reaction. The key aspect of a battery which differentiates it from other oxidation/reduction reactions is that the oxidation and reduction reaction are physically separated. When the reactions are physically separated, a load can be inserted between the two reactions. The electrochemical potential difference between the two batteries corresponds to the voltage of the battery which drives the load, and the exchange of electrons between the two reactions corresponds to the current that passes through the load. The components of a battery, which are shown in the Figures below, and consist of an electrode and electrolyte for both the reduction and oxidation reaction, a means to transfer electrons between the reduction and oxidation reaction (usually this is accomplished by a wire connected to each electrode) and a means to exchange charged ions between the two reactions.

Figure: a

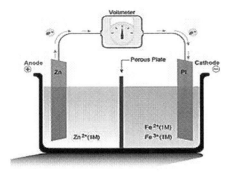

Figure: b

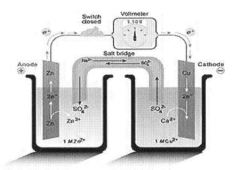

Figure: Schematic of a battery in which (a) the electrolyte of the reduction and oxidation reaction are different and (b) the electrolyte is the same for both reactions.

The key components which determine many of the basic properties of the battery are the materials used for the electrode and electrolyte for both the oxidation and reduction reactions. The electrode is the physical location where the core of the redox reaction – the transfer of electrons – takes place. In many battery systems, including lead acid and alkaline batteries, the electrode is not only where the electron transfer takes places, but is also a component in the chemical reaction that either uses or produces the electron. However, in other battery systems (such as fuel cells) the electrode material is itself inert and is only the site for the electron transfer from one reactant to another. For a discharging battery, the electrode at which the oxidation reaction occurs is called the anode and by definition has a positive voltage, and the electrode at which the reduction reaction occurs is the cathode and is at a negative voltage.

The electrode alone is not sufficient for a redox reaction to take place since a redox reaction involves the interaction of more than a single component. The other chemical components of the reaction are contained in the electrolyte. For many practical battery systems, the electrolyte is an aqueous solution. One reason for having an aqueous solution is the oxidized or reduced form of the electrode exists in an aqueous solution. Further, it is important that the chemical species in the electrolyte be mobile in order that they can move to the site on the electrode where the chemical reaction takes places, and also such that ion species can travel from one electrode to the other.

The current in the battery arises from the transfer of electrons from one electrode to the other. During discharging, the oxidation reaction at the anode generates electrons and a reduction reaction at the cathode using these electrons, and therefore during discharging, electrons flow from the anode to the cathode. The electrons generated or used in the redox reaction can easily be transported between the electrodes via a conventional electrical connection, such as a wire attached to the anode and cathode. However, unlike a conventional electrical circuit, electrons are not the only charge carrier in the circuit. Electrons travel from the anode to the cathode but do not return from the cathode to the anode. Instead, electrical neutrality is maintained by the movement of ions in the electrolyte. If each redox reaction has a different electrolyte, a salt bridge joins the two electrolyte solutions. The direction of the ion movement acts to prevent a charge build-up at either the anode or the cathode. In most practical battery systems, the same electrolyte is used for both the anode and the cathode, and ion transport can take place via the electrolyte itself, eliminating the need for a salt bridge. However, in this case, a separator is also inserted between the anode and the cathode. The separator prevents the anode and cathode from physically touching each other since they are usually in very close physical proximity to one another, and if they were to touch it would short out the battery as the electrons can be transferred directly without flowing through the external circuit and load.

The redox reactions which comprise a particular battery system define many fundamental parameters about the battery system. Other key battery properties, including as battery capacity, charging/discharging performance and other practical considerations are also influenced by the physical configuration of the battery, for example, the amount of material in the battery or the geometry of the electrodes. The following pages describe how battery characteristics – voltage behavior, battery efficiency, battery non-idealities (self-discharge, degradation of battery capacity, etc.) – are dependent on the operation of the redox reactions and the battery configuration.

3.1 Oxidation-Reduction reaction in a battery

Many definitions can be given to oxidation and reduction reactions. In terms of electrochemistry, the following definition is most appropriate, because it let us see how the electrons perform their roles in the chemistry of batteries.

Loss of electrons is oxidation, and gain of electrons is a reduction.

Oxidation and reduction reactions cannot be carried out separately. They have to appear together in a chemical reaction. Thus oxidation and reduction reactions are often called redox reactions. In terms of redox reactions, a reducing agent and an oxidizing agent form a redox couple as they undergo the reaction:

Oxidant + n e⁻ = Reductant

Reductant = Oxidant + n e⁻

An oxidant is an oxidizing reagent, and a reductant is a reducing agent.

reductant | oxidant or *oxidant | reductant*

Two members of the couple are the same element or compound but of different oxidation state.

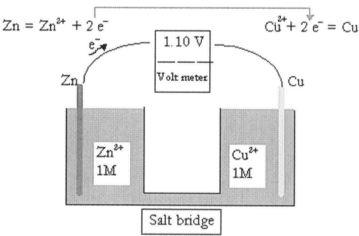

Figure: Copper-Zinc Voltaic Cell

As an introduction to electrochemistry let us take a look at a simple Voltaic cell or a galvanic cell.

When a stick of zinc (Zn) is inserted in a salt solution, there is a tendency for Zn to lose electron according to the reaction,

$Zn = Zn^{2+} + 2 e^-$.

The arrangement of a Zn electrode in a solution containing Zn^{2+} ions is a half cell, which is usually represented by the notation:

$Zn \mid Zn^{2+}$,

Zinc metal and Zn^{2+} ion form a redox couple, Zn^{2+} being the oxidant, and Zn the reductant. The same notation was used to designate a redox couple earlier.

Similarly, when a stick of copper (Cu) is inserted in a copper salt solution, there is also a tendency for Cu to lose electron according to the reaction,

$Cu = Cu^{2+} + 2 e^-$.

This is another half-cell or redox couple: $Cu \mid Cu^{2+}$.

However, the tendency for Zn to lose electron is stronger than that for copper. When the two cells are connected by a salt bridge and an electric conductor as shown to form a closed circuit for electrons and ions to flow, copper ions (Cu^{2+}) actually gains an electron to become copper metal. The reaction and the redox couple are respectively represented below,

$Cu^{2+} + 2 e^- = Cu$,

$Cu^{2+} \mid Cu$.

This arrangement is called a galvanic cell or battery as shown here. In a text form, this battery is represented by,

$Zn \mid Zn^{2+} \mid\mid Cu^{2+} \mid Cu$,

In which the two vertical lines (| |) represent a salt bridge, and a single vertical line (|) represents the boundary between the two phases (metal and solution). Electrons flow through the electric conductors connecting the electrodes and ions flow through the salt bridge. When

$$[Zn^{2+}] = [Cu^{2+}] = 1.0 \text{ M},$$

The voltage between the two terminals has been measured to be 1.100 V for this battery.

A battery is a package of one or more galvanic cells used for the production and storage of electric energy. The simplest battery consists of two half cells, a reduction half-cell, and an oxidation half cell.

Chapter 4: Types of Batteries

Batteries can be broadly classified into two types based on their charging capability and they're built in construction.

Below are the classification of Batteries

- **Primary Battery**

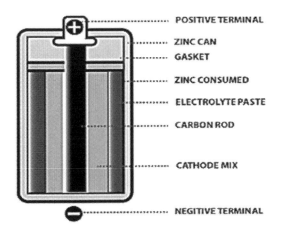

These are batteries where the redox reaction occurs only once, thus rendering the battery dead after a certain period of time. Example, the dry cell batteries we use in our torches, wall clocks or remotes cannot be used once it is exhausted. In such cells, a zinc container acts as an anode and a carbon rod acts as a cathode. A powdered mixture of manganese dioxide and carbon is placed surrounding the cathode. The space left in between the container and the rod is filled with a moist paste of ammonium chloride and zinc chloride. The redox reaction taking place in such a cell is given by,

At anode: $Zn(s) \rightarrow Zn^{2+} (aq) + 2e^-$

At cathode: $2e^- + 2 NH_4^+ (aq) \rightarrow 2 NH_3 (g) + H_2 (g)$

$2 NH_3 (g) + Zn^{2+} (aq) \rightarrow [Zn (NH_3)_2]^{2+} (aq)$

$H_2 (g) + 2 MnO_2 (S) \rightarrow Mn_2O_3 (S) + H_2O (l)$

--

$Zn(s) + 2 NH_4^+ (aq) + 2 MnO_2 (S) \rightarrow [Zn (NH_3)_2]^{2+} (aq) + Mn_2O_3 (S) + H_2O (l)$

- **Secondary Battery**

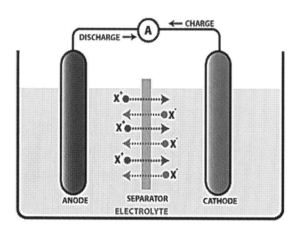

These are batteries that can be recharged after use by passing current through the electrodes in the opposite direction i.e.,

40

from the negative terminal to the positive terminal. For example, a lead storage battery that is used in automobiles and invertors can be recharged a limited number of times. The lead storage battery consists of a lead anode and the cathode is a lead grid packed with lead dioxide. Sulphuric acid with a concentration of 38% is used as an electrolyte. The redox reaction involved in this process is can be given as,

At anode: $Pb \longrightarrow Pb^{2+} + 2\ e^-$

$Pb + SO_4^{2-} \longrightarrow PbSO_4\ (electrode) + 2\ e^-$

At cathode: $2\ e^- + PbO_2 + 4\ H^+ \longrightarrow Pb^{2+} + 2\ H_2O$

$2\ e^- + PbO_2 + 4\ H^+ + SO_4^{2-} \longrightarrow PbSO_4\ (electrode) + 2\ H_2O$

In order to recharge these batteries, the charge is transferred in the opposite direction and the reaction is reversed, thus converting $PbSO_4$ back to Pb and PbO_2.

Chapter 5: Types of Cell

Many types of electrochemical cells have been produced, with varying chemical processes and designs, including galvanic cells, electrolytic cells, fuel cells, flow cells and voltaic piles.

- **Wet Cell**

A wet cell battery has a liquid electrolyte. Other names are flooded cell since the liquid covers all internal parts, or vented cell since gases produced during operation can escape to the air. Wet cells were a precursor to dry cells and are commonly used as a learning tool for electrochemistry. They can be built with common laboratory supplies, such as beakers, for demonstrations of how electrochemical cells work. A particular type of wet cell known as a concentration cell is important in understanding corrosion. Wet cells may be primary cells (non-rechargeable) or secondary cells (rechargeable). Originally, all practical primary batteries such as the Daniell cell were built as open-top glass jar wet cells. Other primary wet cells are the Leclanche cell, Grove cell, Bunsen cell, Chromic acid cell, Clark cell, and Weston cell. The Leclanche cell chemistry was adapted to the first dry cells. Wet cells are still used in automobile batteries and in the industry for standby power for switchgear, telecommunication or large uninterruptible power supplies, but in many places, batteries with gel cells have been used instead. These applications commonly use lead–acid or nickel–cadmium cells.

- **Dry Cell**

A dry cell uses a paste electrolyte, with only enough moisture to allow current to flow. Unlike a wet cell, a dry cell can operate in any orientation without spilling, as it contains no free liquid, making it suitable for portable equipment. By comparison, the first wet cells were typically fragile glass containers with lead rods hanging from the open top and needed careful handling to avoid spillage. Lead–acid batteries did not achieve the safety and portability of the dry cell until the development of the gel battery.

A common dry cell is a zinc-carbon battery, sometimes called the dry Leclanché cell, with a nominal voltage of 1.5 volts, the same as the alkaline battery (since both use the same zinc-manganese dioxide combination). A standard dry cell comprises a zinc anode, usually in the form of a cylindrical pot, with a carbon cathode in the form of a central rod. The electrolyte is ammonium chloride in the form of a paste next to the zinc anode. The remaining space between the electrolyte and carbon cathode is taken up by a second paste consisting of ammonium chloride and manganese dioxide, the latter acting as a depolarizer. In some designs, the ammonium chloride is replaced by zinc chloride.

- **Molten Salt**

Molten salt batteries are primary or secondary batteries that use a molten salt as the electrolyte. They operate at high temperatures and must be well insulated to retain heat.

- **Reserve Battery**

A reserve battery can be stored unassembled (inactivated and supplying no power) for a long period (perhaps years). When the battery is needed, then it is assembled (e.g., by adding electrolyte); once assembled, the battery is charged and ready to work. For example, a battery for an electronic artillery fuse might be activated by the impact of firing a gun. The acceleration breaks a capsule of electrolyte that activates the battery and powers the fuze's circuits. Reserve batteries are usually designed for a short service life (seconds or minutes) after long storage (years). A water-activated battery for oceanographic instruments or military applications becomes activated on immersion in water.

Chapter 6: Cell Performance

A battery's characteristics may vary overload cycle, overcharge cycle, and over a lifetime due to many factors including internal chemistry, current drain, and temperature. At low temperatures, a battery cannot deliver as much power. As such, in cold climates, some car owners install battery warmers, which are small electric heating pads that keep the car battery warm.

6.1 Capacity and Discharge

A battery's capacity is the amount of electric charge it can deliver at the rated voltage. The more electrode material contained in the cell the greater its capacity. A small cell has less capacity than a larger cell with the same chemistry, although they develop the same open-circuit voltage. Capacity is measured in units such as amp-hour. The rated capacity of a battery is usually expressed as the product of 20 hours multiplied by the current that a new battery can consistently supply for 20 hours at 68 °F (20 °C) while remaining above a specified terminal voltage per cell. For example, a battery rated at 100 Ah can deliver 5 A over a 20-hour period at room temperature. The fraction of the stored charge that a battery can deliver depends on multiple factors, including battery chemistry, the rate at which the charge is delivered (current), the required terminal voltage, the storage period, ambient temperature and other factors.

The higher the discharge rate, the lower the capacity. The relationship between current, discharge time and capacity for a lead acid battery is approximated (over a typical range of current values) by Peukert's law:

$t = Q_P/I^k$

Where,

Q_P is the capacity when discharged at a rate of 1 amp.

t is the amount of time (in hours) that a battery can sustain.

k is a constant around.

Chapter 7: C Rate

Charge and discharge rates of a battery are governed by C-rates. The capacity of a battery is commonly rated at 1C, meaning that a fully charged battery rated at 1Ah should provide 1A for one hour. The same battery discharging at 0.5C should provide 500mA for two hours, and at 2C it delivers 2A for 30 minutes. Losses at fast discharges reduce the discharge time and these losses also affect charge times.

A C-rate of 1C is also known as a one-hour discharge; 0.5C or C/2 is a two-hour discharge and 0.2C or C/5 is a 5-hour discharge. Some high-performance batteries can be charged and discharged above 1C with moderate stress. The table illustrates typical times at various C-rates.

C-rate	Time
5C	12 min
2C	30 min
1C	1h
0.5C or C/2	2h
0.2C or C/5	5h
0.1C or C/10	10h
0.05C or C/20	20h

Table: C-rate and service times when charging and discharging batteries of 1Ah (1,000mAh)

The battery capacity, or the amount of energy a battery can hold, can be measured with a battery analyzer. The analyzer discharges the battery at a calibrated current while measuring the time until the end-of-discharge voltage is reached. For lead acid, the end-of-discharge is typically 1.75V/cell, for NiCd/NiMH 1.0V/cell and for Li-ion 3.0V/cell. If a 1Ah battery provides 1A for one hour, an analyzer displaying the results in a percentage of the nominal rating will show 100 percent. If the discharge lasts 30 minutes before reaching the end-of-discharge cut-off voltage, then the battery has a capacity of 50 percent. A new battery is sometimes overrated and can produce more than 100 percent capacity; others are underrated and never reach 100 percent, even after priming.

When discharging a battery with a battery analyzer capable of applying different C rates, a higher C rate will produce a lower capacity reading and vice versa. By discharging the 1Ah battery at the faster 2C-rate, or 2A, the battery should ideally deliver the full capacity in 30 minutes. The sum should be the same since the identical amount of energy is dispensed over a shorter time. In reality, internal losses turn some of the energy into heat and lower the resulting capacity to about 95 percent or less. Discharging the same battery at 0.5C, or 500mA over 2 hours, will likely increase the capacity to above 100 percent.

To obtain a reasonably good capacity reading, manufacturers commonly rate alkaline and lead-acid batteries at a very low 0.05C or a 20-hour discharge. Even at this slow discharge rate, lead-acid seldom attain a 100 percent capacity as the batteries are overrated. Manufacturers provide capacity offsets to adjust for the discrepancies if discharged at a higher C rate than specified. The Figure will illustrate the discharge times of a lead acid battery at various loads expressed in C-rate.

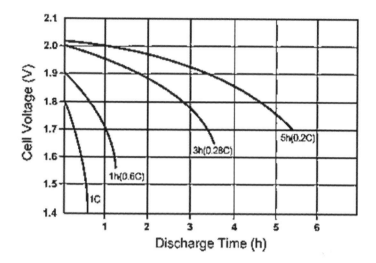

Figure: Typical discharge curves of lead acid as a function of C-rate.

Small Batteries are rated at 1C discharge rate.

While lead- and nickel-based batteries can be discharged at a high rate, the protection circuit prevents the Li-ion Energy Cell from discharging above 1C. The Power Cell with nickel, manganese and/or phosphate active material can tolerate discharge rates of up to 10C and the current threshold is set higher accordingly.

Chapter 8: Factors affecting battery life

Batteries have limited life, usually showing a slow degradation of capacity until they reach 80 percent of their initial rating, followed by a comparatively rapid failure. Regardless of how or where a UPS is deployed, and what size it is, there are four primary factors that affect battery life: ambient temperature, battery chemistry, cycling, and service.

Here a few other factors.

- **Ambient Temperature**

The rated capacity of a battery is based on an ambient temperature of 25°C (77°F). It's important to realize that any variation from this operating temperature can alter the battery's performance and shorten its expected life. To help determine battery life in relation to temperature, remember that for every 8.3°C (15°F) average annual temperature above 25°C (77°F), the life of the battery is reduced by 50%.

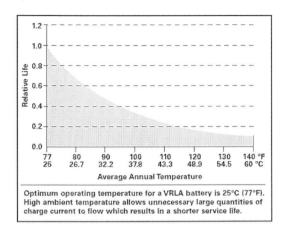

Optimum operating temperature for a VRLA battery is 25°C (77°F). High ambient temperature allows unnecessary large quantities of charge current to flow which results in a shorter service life.

- **Battery Chemistry**

UPS batteries are electrochemical devices whose ability to store and deliver power slowly decreases over time. Even if you follow all the guidelines for proper storage, usage, and maintenance, batteries still require replacement after a certain period of time.

- **Cycling**

During a utility power failure, a UPS operates on battery power. Once utility power is restored, or a switch to generator power is complete, the battery is recharged for future use. This is called a discharge cycle. At installation, the battery is at 100 percent of rated capacity. Each discharge and subsequent recharge reduces its relative capacity by a small percentage. The length of the discharge cycle determines the reduction in battery capacity. Lead-acid chemistry, like others used in rechargeable batteries, can only undergo a maximum number of discharge/recharge cycles before the chemistry is depleted. Once the chemistry is depleted, the cells fail and the battery must be replaced.

- **Maintainance**

   Battery service and maintenance are critical to UPS reliability. A gradual decrease in battery life can be monitored and evaluated through voltage checks, load testing or monitoring. Periodic preventive maintenance extends battery string life by preventing loose connections, removing corrosion and identifying bad batteries before they can affect the rest of the string. Even though sealed batteries are sometimes referred to as maintenance-free, they still require scheduled maintenance and service. Maintenance-free simply refers to the fact that they don't require fluid. Without regular maintenance, your UPS battery may experience heat-generating resistance at the terminals, improper loading, reduced protection and premature failure. With proper maintenance, the end of battery life can be accurately estimated and replacements scheduled without unexpected downtime or loss of backup power.

Chapter 9: The selection of the right Battery for the desired application

The one thing to remember about battery selection is that there is no such thing as a perfect battery that works for every application. Selecting the right battery for your application is about identifying the most important battery metrics and trading these off against others. For instance, if you need a lot of power for your application, cell internal resistance needs to be minimized, and this is often done by increasing electrode surface area. But this also increases inactive components such as current collectors and conductive aid, so energy density is traded off to gain power.

While your actual design goals on the battery may be lofty, you could have to give up some things in order to gain others when it comes to actual battery performance.

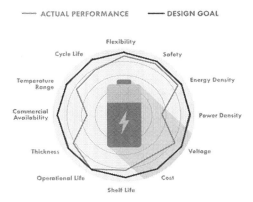

- **Primary vs Secondary**

One of the first choices in battery selection is to decide whether the application requires primary (single use) or secondary (rechargeable) batteries. For the most part, this is an easy decision for the designer. Applications with occasional intermittent use (such as a smoke alarm, a toy or a flashlight), and disposable applications in which charging becomes impractical warrant the use of a primary battery. Hearing aids, watches (smartwatches being an exception), greeting cards and pacemakers are good examples. If the battery is to be used continuously and for long stretches of time, such as in a laptop, a cell phone or a smartwatch a rechargeable battery is more suitable. Primary batteries have a much lower rate of self-discharge - an attractive feature when charging is not possible or practical before first use. Secondary batteries tend to lose energy at a higher rate. This is less important in most applications because of the ability to recharge.

- **Energy vs Power**

The runtime of a battery is dictated by the battery capacity expressed in mAh or Ah and is the discharge current that a battery can provide over time.

When comparing batteries of different chemistry, it is useful to look at the energy content. To obtain the energy content of a battery, multiply the battery capacity in Ah by the voltage to obtain energy in Wh. For instance, a nickel-metal hydride battery with 1.2 V, and a lithium-ion battery with 3.2 V may have the same capacity, but the higher voltage of the lithium-ion would increase the energy.

The open circuit voltage is commonly used in energy calculations (i.e. battery voltage when not connected to a load). However, both the capacity and energy are both heavily dependent on the drain rate. Theoretical capacity is dictated only by active electrode materials (chemistry) and active mass. Yet, practical batteries achieve only a fraction of the theoretical numbers due to the presence of inactive materials and kinetic limitations, which prevent full use of active materials and buildup of discharge products on the electrodes.

Battery manufacturers often specify capacity at a given discharge rate, temperature, and cut-off voltage. The specified capacity will depend on all three factors. When comparing manufacturer capacity ratings, make sure you look at drain rates in particular. A battery that appears to have a high capacity on a spec sheet may actually perform poorly if the current drain for the application is higher. For instance, a battery rated at 2 Ah for a 20-hour discharge cannot deliver 2 A for 1 hour, but will only provide a fraction of the capacity.

Batteries with high power provide rapid discharge capability at high drain rates such as in power tools or automobile starter battery applications. Typically, high power batteries have low energy densities.

A good analogy for power versus energy is to think of a bucket with a spout. A larger bucket can hold more water and is akin to a battery with high energy. The opening or spout size from which the water leaves the bucket is akin to power – the higher the power, the higher the drain rate. To increase energy, you would typically increase the battery size (for a given chemistry), but to increase power you decrease internal resistance. Cell construction plays a huge part in obtaining batteries with high power density.

- **Voltage**

Battery operating voltage is another important consideration and is dictated by the electrode materials used. A useful battery classification here is to consider aqueous or water-based batteries versus lithium-based chemistries. Lead acid, Zinc-carbon and Nickel metal hydride all use water-based electrolytes and have nominal voltages ranging from 1.2 to 2 V. Lithium based batteries, on the other hand, use organic electrolytes and have nominal voltages of 3.2 to 4 V (both primary and secondary).

Many electronic components operate at a minimum voltage of 3 V. The higher operating voltage of lithium-based chemistries allows a single cell to be used rather than two or three aqueous based cells in series to make up the desired voltage.

Another thing to note is that some battery chemistries such as Zinc MnO_2 have a sloping discharge curve, while others have a flat profile.

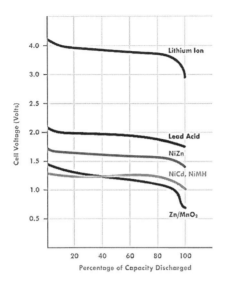

Figure: Voltage Plot Based on Battery Chemistry

- **Temperature Range**

Battery chemistry dictates the temperature range of the application. For instance, aqueous electrolyte based Zinc-carbon cells cannot be used below 0°C. Alkaline cells also exhibit a sharp decline in capacity at these temperatures, although less than Zinc-carbon. Lithium primary batteries with an organic electrolyte can be operated up to -40°C but with a significant drop in performance.

In rechargeable applications, lithium-ion batteries can be charged at a maximum rate only within a narrow window of about 20° to 45°C. Beyond this temperature range, lower currents/voltages need to be used, resulting in longer charging times. At temperatures below 5° or 10°C, a trickle charge may be required in order to prevent the dreaded lithium dendritic plating problem, which increases the risk of thermal runaway (we have all heard of exploding Lithium based batteries which could happen as a result of overcharging, low or high-temperature charging or short-circuiting from contaminants).

- **Shelf life**

This refers to how long a battery will sit in a storeroom or on a shelf before it is used. Primary batteries have much longer shelf lives than secondary. However, shelf life is generally more important for primary batteries because secondary batteries have the ability to be recharged. An exception is when recharging is not practical.

- **Chemistry**

Many of the properties listed above are dictated by cell chemistry. We will discuss commonly available battery chemistries in the next part of this blog series.

- **Physical size and shape**

Batteries are typically available in the following size formats: button/coin cells, cylindrical cells, prismatic cells, and pouch cells (most of them in standardized formats).

- **Cost**

There are times when you may need to pass up a battery with better performance characteristics because the application is very cost sensitive. This is especially true for high volume disposable applications.

- **Transportation & disposal regulations**

Transportation of lithium-based batteries is regulated. Disposal of certain battery chemistries is also regulated. This may be a consideration for high volume applications.

Chapter 10: Lithium-ion Battery

Li-ion batteries have an unmatchable combination of high energy and power density, making it the technology of choice for portable electronics, power tools, and hybrid/full electric vehicles. If electric vehicles replace the majority of gasoline powered transportation, Li-ion batteries will significantly reduce greenhouse gas emissions. The high energy efficiency of Li-ion batteries may also allow their use in various electric grid applications, including improving the quality of energy harvested from wind, solar, geothermal and other renewable sources, thus contributing to their more widespread use and building an energy-sustainable economy. Therefore Li-ion batteries are of intense interest from both industry and government funding agencies, and research in this field has abounded in the recent years.

Since Li-ion batteries are the first choice source of portable electrochemical energy storage, improving their cost and performance can greatly expand their applications and enable new technologies which depend on energy storage. A great volume of research in Li-ion batteries has thus far been in electrode materials. Electrodes with higher rate capability, higher charge capacity, and sufficiently high voltage can improve the energy and power densities of Lwebatteries and make them smaller and cheaper. However, this is only true assuming that the material itself is not too expensive or rare.

10.1 History and development

Lithium is one of the lightest elements in the periodic table and it has one of the largest electrochemical potentials, therefore this combination produces some of the highest possible voltages in the most compact and lightest volumes.

This is the basis for the lithium-ion battery. In this new battery, lithium is combined with a transition metal – such as cobalt, nickel, manganese or iron – and oxygen to form the cathode. During recharging when a voltage is applied, the positively charged lithium-ion from the cathode migrates to the graphite anode and becomes lithium metal, Because lithium has a strong electrochemical driving force to be oxidised if allowed, it migrates back to the cathode to become a Li+ ion again and gives up its electron back to the cobalt ion. The movement of electrons in the circuit gives us a current that we can use. Depending on the transition metal used in the lithium-ion battery, the cell can have a higher capacity but can be more reactive and susceptible to a phenomenon known as thermal runaway.

In the case of lithium cobalt oxide ($LiCoO_2$) batteries made by Sony in the 1990s, this led to many such batteries catching fire. The possibility of making battery cathodes from nano-scale material and hence more reactive was out of the question.

But in the 1990s Goodenough again made a huge leap in battery technology by introducing a stable lithium-ion cathode based on lithium iron and phosphate.

This cathode is thermally stable. It also means that nano-scale lithium iron phosphate ($LiFePO_4$) or lithium ferrophosphate (LFP) materials can now be made safely into large format cells that can be rapidly charged and discharged. Many new applications now exist for these new cells, from power tools to hybrid and electric vehicle. Perhaps the most important application will be the storage of domestic electric energy for households.

10.2 Why Li-ion Battery?

Lithium is the lightest of all metals, has the greatest electrochemical potential and provides the largest energy density for weight. The energy density of lithium-ion is typically twice that of the standard nickel-cadmium. There is potential for higher energy densities. The load characteristics are reasonably good and behave similarly to nickel-cadmium in terms of discharge. The high cell voltage of 3.6 volts allows battery pack designs with only one cell. Most of today's mobile phones run on a single cell. A nickel-based pack would require three 1.2-volt cells connected in series.

Lithium-ion is a low maintenance battery, an advantage that most other chemistries cannot claim. There is no memory and no scheduled cycling is required to prolong the battery's life. In addition, the self-discharge is less than half compared to nickel-cadmium, making lithium-ion well suited for modern fuel gauge applications. Lithium-ion cells cause little harm when disposed of.

Manufacturers are constantly improving lithium-ion. New and enhanced chemical combinations are introduced every six months or so. With such rapid progress, it is difficult to assess how well the revised battery will age.

Some rechargeable cells need to be primed when they receive their first charge. There is no requirement for this with lithium-ion cells and batteries.

There are several types of lithium-ion cell available. This advantage of lithium-ion batteries can mean that the right technology can be used for the particular application needed. Some forms of lithium-ion battery provide a high current density and are ideal for consumer mobile electronic equipment. Others are able to provide much higher current levels and are ideal for power tools and electric vehicles.

Chapter 11: Battery Pack

Battery packs are any number of individual batteries arranged in series or parallel to provide the required power to electronic devices. The most typical type of battery used in battery packs is lithium-ion due to their high power density. The application of battery packs is wide-ranging from phones to lawn mowers to automobiles

11.1 Why use Battery Pack

Battery cells are like eggs. Cells come in fixed voltages and capacities. If you need more voltage, you can deal with multiples of the cell voltage. You can't get half an egg, and you can't get half a cell, at least in voltage. Cell capacities do vary, particularly with a supplier like Power Stream that has a great variety of cell sizes available, but voltages don't. All NiCad or NiMH cells are 1.2 volts nominal, lead acid is 2.0 volts nominal and the various lithium technologies are about 3.6 volts per cell. If you need more voltage you have to add them in series, if you need less voltage you need some kind of voltage regulator or DC/DC converter.

If you need more current than a single cell can supply you may need to put cells in parallel. If you need more capacity to give longer run time you may also put cells in parallel.

Many times the physical configuration makes it more attractive to use many small cells rather than a few large cells since a large block is harder to fit than several small subunits.

11.2 Battery Pack Design overview

A battery pack is a system of multiple components and functions and its design involves the application of knowledge and practice in the electrochemical, electrical, mechanical, thermodynamic, and control fields. The following sections summarize the various stages of a battery pack design

- The first step in the design of the pack is to determine the configuration of cells, i.e. how many cells overall, how many are in series, and how many are in parallel. This is the foundation of the design process since all other design decisions follow from the cell configuration.

- The second step is to design a mechanical structure around the cells to support and protect them. This step requires knowledge of electrical, mechanical and thermodynamic requirements and properties of the cells, application, and the materials used in the pack.

- The third step is to design the protection of the cells, particularly electrical protection. The pack must be protected from inadvertent short circuits internal and external to the pack as well as excessive charging and discharging imposed on its terminals.

- The fourth step is to design a control system that monitors and manages the cells, keeping them from being damaged and maintaining the pack at peak performance.

11.3 Cell Configuration

The ultimate shape and dimensions of the battery pack are mostly governed by the cavity which is planned to house it within the intended application. This, in turn, dictates the possible cell sizes and layouts which can be used. Prismatic cells provide the best space utilization, however, cylindrical cells provide simpler cooling options for high power batteries. The use of pouch cells provides the product designer more freedom in specifying the shape of the battery cavity permitting very compact designs.

The orientation of the cells is designed to minimize the interconnections between the cells.

11.4 Configuration of the battery pack

Custom battery pack configurations are how the individual battery cells are connected together to create a complete battery pack assembly. There are many different battery pack configurations that need to be considered when designing a battery pack for your end product.

Here are few standard battery pack configurations.

- **Linear or F type**

Note that the straps will both come off the top when there is an even number of cells, and one off the top, the other off the bottom when there is an odd number of cells.

"F" Type Construction

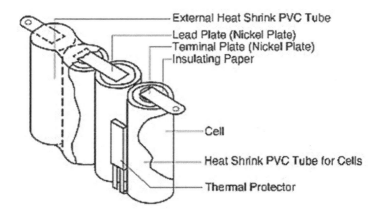

External Heat Shrink PVC Tube
Lead Plate (Nickel Plate)
Terminal Plate (Nickel Plate)
Insulating Paper

Cell

Heat Shrink PVC Tube for Cells

Thermal Protector

Figure: F Type battery configuration

- **Multiple row cells (Cubic or composed F type)**

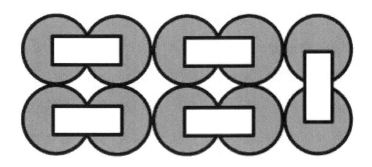

When multiple rows of F Type Battery Pack is connected at the ends of each row, this comprises to form a multiple row cell battery pack.

- **Linear or L type cell**

This is a stack of cells end to end. These are usually constructed by standing two cells side-by-side and welding a nickel strip across the terminals. The cells are bent end to end by bending the nickel strip in "U" shape.

"L" Type Construction

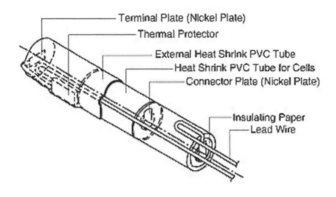

Figure: L Type Battery configuration

11.5 Battery pack structural design

A well-designed battery pack protects and replicates the individual cell performance of multiple cells in the pack. It provides mechanical protection and integrity, thermal stability, and electrical protection and performance. The electrical interconnections, mechanical supports, and thermodynamic systems are all essential elements of the battery pack's structural design.

The battery casing has to provide the mechanical and electrical interfaces to the product it is designed to power as well as to contain all the components.

The simplest and least expensive packaging for small batteries is shrink wrap or vacuum formed plastic. These solutions are only possible if the battery is intended to be completely enclosed by the finished product.

Figure: Battery pack mould.

Injection molded plastics are used to provide more precision packs. For enclosed packs designs using a minimum of materials are based around which a plastic frame holds the components in place thus minimizing the cost, the weight and the size of the pack. The overall product cost can be further reduced by using insert moldings in which the interconnection strips and the terminals are molded into the plastic parts to eliminate both materials and assembly costs. Over moulding may also be used to encapsulate and protect small components or sub-assemblies.

In some designs, the battery pack forms part of the outer case of the end product. The colors and textures of the plastic must match the plastics of the rest of the product even though they may come from a completely different supplier. These designs are usually required to incorporate a mechanical latch to hold the battery in place. Again this latch, as well as the terminals, must interface with plastic parts from a different supplier so high precision and tight tolerances are essential. ABS polymers are the materials typically used for this purpose.

Batteries for traction applications are usually very large and heavy and subject to large physical forces as well as vibrations so substantial fixings are required to hold the cells in place. This is particularly necessary for batteries made up from pouch cells which are vulnerable to physical damage. Automotive battery packs must also withstand abuse and possible accidental damage so metal casings will normally be specified. The metal pack casing also serves to confine any incendiary event resulting from the failure of a cell or cells within the battery and to provide a measure of protection for the user. At the same time, the case must also protect the cells and the electronics from the harsh operating environments of temperature extremes, water ingress, humidity and vibration in which these batteries work.

Usually, the complete pack is replaced when the battery has reached the end of its useful life. In certain circumstances, however, for instance, when the pack incorporates a lot of electronic circuits, it may be desirable to design the pack such that the cells within the pack can be replaced. If the design requires provision for replacement of the cells the casing of the battery pack must be designed to clip or screw together. Normally the parts of the plastic housing will be ultrasonically welded together both for security and for low cost as well as to prevent unauthorized tampering with the cells and the electronics.

11.6 Battery pack cell protection

As battery technology and form factors for electronic devices expand beyond traditional cylindrical cells, Lithium based batteries are in increased demand due to their high energy density, small form factors, and design flexibility. Although some Li-ion cylindrical cells contain a PTC as a basic protection against current surges, popular Lithium polymer cells do not contain PTCs, and as such, additional consideration must be applied in order to prevent premature failure caused by misuse and or improper handling.

11.6.1 Need for protection

Battery packs containing Li-ion cells require a mandatory protection circuit or CID (circuit interrupt device) to assure safety. In addition to cell level safeguards, an external protection circuit or what is commonly known as PCM (Protection Circuit Module) is often implemented on battery packs to prevent thermal runaway resulting either from Overcharge, Over-discharge, Over-voltage, Over-current, and Short-circuit condition. Since Lithium based batteries contain very high specific energy per volume, an unprotected cell or battery pack can potentially result in costly and irreversible damage.

Here are a few conditions from which Battery packs must be protected:

• Overcharge Conditions

Various battery chemistries require specific charging profiles to optimize performance and prevent safety issues during charge. Generally, almost all Li-ion battery chargers use a constant current/constant voltage charging algorithm. Once the charger enters constant voltage mode it is important to ensure the charge does not exceed the maximum level allowed to avoid exposing them to overcharge conditions as it can cause excessive internal temperature rise and lead to premature failure.

Causes of cell or battery pack overcharge condition.

a)   Faulty charger: Charger fails to stop or limit the supply voltage once it is fully charged

b)   Improper Use: Cell or battery is charged using the non-compatible charger

• Over-current Conditions

Over-current conditions occur when Li-ion cell or battery pack is charged or discharged at a much higher current than its design set by cell a manufacturer. For example, if the manufacturer states a Li-ion 18650 cell is only rated for 2.0A maximum continuous discharge current but the user decides to neglect this warning and applies a continuous load of 4.0A. The cell has now gone into what is known as over-current condition and can cause the internal temperature to rise from the chemical reaction and may lead to swelling or rupturing of cells and risk of damaging the battery. To help prevent this condition the end-user must always adhere to the manufacturer's cell or battery specification.

• Short circuit conditions

Accidental short circuits can occur when exposed positive and negative terminals come into contact with a metal object such as a keychain or poorly handled lead wires, which will lead to a rapid rise in the cell internal temperature and result in performance degradation as well as swelling of cells. Test results on unprotected lithium cell, from testing laboratories such UL and Intertek, has shown that temperatures can reach in excess of 600°C or 1112°F during this type of event and may lead to venting of toxic and highly flammable gases. Once ignited, it can propagate to other cells or flammable objects and lead to irreversible damage.

Causes for the short circuit:

a)   Exposed positive and negative terminals come into contact with metal objects

b)   Reversed polarity

c)   Poor manufacturing or assembly

• Over-discharge condition

Typical rechargeable lithium cells can safely operate down to 2.75V/cell. However, when an unprotected lithium cell is discharged past the minimum voltage level you run the risk of damaging the cell and ultimately lead to degraded cycle-life, unstable voltage characteristics and swelling of cells from the internal chemical reaction. Generally, a protection circuit is designed with some extra buffer, usually in the +0.25~0.40V range from the cell manufacturer's minimum voltage, in order to prevent prematurely triggering the discharge cut-off voltage.

Common causes of over discharge conditions:

a)   Host device minimum operating voltage is below cell's discharge cut-off Voltage

b)   Improperly set discharge cut-off Voltage

c)   Poorly implemented Protection Circuit Module

11.6.2 Protection circuits

The most basic safety device in a battery is a fuse that opens on high current. Some fuses open permanently and render the battery useless; others are more forgiving and reset. The positive thermal coefficient (PTC) is such a re-settable device that creates high resistance to excess current and reverts back to the low ON position when the condition normalizes. Further layers of safeguards are solid-state switches that measure the current and voltage and disconnect the circuit if the values are too high. The protection circuits of Li-ion work on this on/off basis.

11.6.3 DIY Battery Pack & Protection circuit.

Ref: Industructables.com

For this project, we will be using 18650 Batteries, the 18650 (18mm diameter and 65mm length) battery is a size classification of lithium-ion batteries. It is the same shape, but a bit larger than an AA battery. AA batteries, by comparison, are sometimes called 14500 batteries because they have a 14mm diameter and 50mm height.

- **Step 1: Parts, tools, and safety required**

Parts Required:

1. 18650 Battery
2. BMS
3. Ni Strips
4. Battery Level Indicator
5. Rocker Switch
6. DC Jack
7. 18650 Battery Holder
8. 3M x 10mm Screws

Tools Used

1. Spot Welder
2. Wire Stripper/ Cutter
3. Hot Air Blower
4. Multimeter
5. Li-Ion Charger

Safety Equipment:

1. Safety Googles

2.   Electrical Gloves

- **Step 2: Selecting the rite 18650 cell for the Battery Pack**

You will find many types of 18650 cells in the market in the price range from ₹150 to ₹900 per piece, but which are the best? We will highly recommend buying 18650 cells from branded companies like Panasonic, Samsung, Sanyo, and LG. These cells that have well-documented performance characteristics and excellent quality control. Reputed brand 18650 cells are generally costly, but if you consider for long time use then they are worth to have it.

Don't buy any cells with the word FIRE in the name of Ultrafire, Surefire, and Trustfire. In reality, these cells are just factory rejects, purchased by companies like Ultrafire and repackaged in their own branded cover. Many used batteries are re-wrapped as new and white-labeled. They sell the battery by marking capacity up to 5000mAh, but in actual their capacity is in between 1000 to 2000 mAh. Another major problem with these cheap 18650 cells is that high risk of explosion when overheated during the charging or discharging.

In this project, we will use green Panasonic 18650B cells of capacity 3400 mAh

Figure: NCR18650B Battery

• Step 3: Choosing the Battery Strip

To make the battery pack, you have to connect the 18650 cells together by means of Nickel strips or thick wire. Generally, Nickel strips are widely used for this. In general two types of nickel, strips are available in the market: nickel-plated steel strips and pure nickel strips. We will suggest buying the pure nickel. It is a little bit costlier than the nickel plated steel, but it has much lower resistance. Low resistance means, less heat generation during the charging and discharging, which leads to longer useful battery life.

Figure: Ni strip

- **Step 4: Soldering**

You can solder the nickel tabs to the cell by following these precaution and tricks:

> 1.   To minimize the contact time of your soldering iron on the cell, make sure the surface is scuffed up sufficiently and you use plenty of flux to allow for fast solder flow.
>
> 2.   It is better to have a good quality high wattage (min 80W) iron with good thermal capacity so it can deliver the heat to the joint quickly so you don't have to hold the iron to the battery for ages and let the heat seep into it, causing damage to the battery.

Figure: Soldering the Battery Pack

- **Step 5: Check the Cell voltage**

Before connecting the cells in parallel, first, check the individual cell voltages. For paralleling the cells, the voltage of each cell should be near to each other, otherwise, a high amount of current will flow from the cell with the higher voltage to the cell with lower voltage. This can damage the cells and even result in a fire on rare occasions.

If you are using brand new cells, the cell voltage is near 3.5 V to 3.7 V, you can join them together without worrying much. But if you are going to use old laptop battery, be sure the cells voltage are nearly same, or else charge the cells to the same voltage level by using a good Li-Ion Battery Charger.

Figure: Checking individual cell voltage using Multimeter

- **Step 6: Battery Pack capacity and voltage**

To make the battery pack, you have to first finalize the nominal voltage and capacity of the pack. Either it will be in term of Volt, mAh/ Ah or Wh. You have to connect the cells in parallel to reach the desired capacity (mAh) and connect such parallel group in series to achieve the nominal voltage (Volt).

For this project let the requirement be: 11.1 V and 17 Ah Battery Pack

Specification of 18650 Cells Used: 3.7V and 3400 mAh

Capacity (mAh):

The desired capacity of the battery pack = 17 AH or 17000 mAh.

The capacity of each cell = 3400 mAh

No of cells required for parallel connection = 17000 / 3400 = 5 no's

Commonly cells in parallel are abbreviated in term of 'P', so this pack will be known as a "5P pack". When 5 cells are connected in parallel, ultimately you made a single cell with higher capacity (i.e. 4.2V, 17000 mAh)

Voltage (Volt):

The desired nominal voltage of the battery pack is 11.1V.

The nominal voltage of each cell = 3.7 V

No of cells required for series connection = 11.1 /3.7 = 3 no's

Commonly cells in series are abbreviated in term of 'S', so this pack will be known as a "3S pack".

So we have to connect the 3 parallel groups (5 cells in each group) in series to make the battery pack.

The final pack configuration is designated as "3S5P pack" with a final specification of 11.1V, 17AH.

- **Step 7: Assembling the cells**

From the previous step, it is clear that our battery pack is made up of 3 parallel groups connected in series (3 x 3.7V = 11.1V) and each parallel group has 5 cells (3400 mAh x 5 = 17000 mAh).Now we have to arrange the 15 cells properly for making the electrical connection among them and with the BMS board.

Place the first parallel group of cells (5 no's) positive side up, then place the second parallel group negative side up and then finally the last parallel group positive side up. For better understanding, you can see the above picture.

You can assemble the cells to make the pack by using hot glue or by using plastic 18650 battery holder. I used plastic 18650 cell holders or spacers to assemble the 15 cells. The main advantages of using this cell holder are

1. You can make the custom pack of any size according to your requirement. It's like a solving a puzzle.

2. It provides space between the cells, which allow fresh air to pass and the battery gets cooled easily.

3. It makes your battery pack solid and reliable.

4. It provides safety anti-vibration to your battery pack

- **Step 8: Solder or spot weld the Ni-strip**

Cut the nickel strips:

Lay your nickel strip on top of the 5 cells (parallel), ensuring that it covers all cells terminals, leave 10mm excess strips for connecting it to the BMS and then cut it. For series connection cut small nickel strips as shown in the Figure. You will need four long strips for parallel connection and 10 small strips for series connections.

Connect the first parallel group negative terminal to the positive terminal of the second group and the negative terminal of the second group to the positive terminal of the third group.

Weld the Battery Strips:

This spot welder can be used to weld the pure nickel as well as nickel plated steel strips. You have to adjust the welder pulse and current knob according to the thickness of the nickel strips.

For 0.15 mm nickel strips, press the pulse knob 4P and current knob to 4-5.Similarly, for 0.2 mm nickel strip, press the pulse knob 4P, 6P and current knob to 7-8.Make sure the welding pen is compressed with the nickel strip and battery terminal, then press the foot switch. You will notice a small spark and two dot mark on the strip.

Successful Welding:

You can check the weld quality by pulling on the nickel strip. If it doesn't come off with hand pressure or requires a lot of strength, then it's a good weld. If you can easily peel it off, then you have to increase the current.

- ## Step 9: Adding the BMS

A battery management system (BMS) is an electronic system that manages a lithium battery pack and the main functionalities are

1. Monitors all of the parallel groups in the battery pack and disconnect it from the input power source when fully charged (near 4.2V)

2. Balance all the cells voltage equally

3. Doesn't allow the pack from over-discharged.

The two important parameter required to buy a BMS are:

a) Number of cells in series - like 2S / 3S / 4S
b) Maximum discharge Current - like 10A/ 20A /25A /30A

For this project, I have used a 3S and 25A BMS board. These are the specifications of that BMS:

Overvoltage range: 4.25~4.35V ± 0.05V

Over-discharge voltage range: 2.3~3.0V ± 0.05V

Maximum operating current: 0~25A

Working temperature: -40°C ~ +50°C

How to Connect?

Connect the BMS as shown in the wiring diagram. The BMS has four soldering pads: B-, B1, B2, and B+. You have to connect the first parallel group negative terminal bus to the B- and positive terminal bus to the B1. Similarly the third parallel group negative terminal bus to the B2 and positive terminal bus to the B+.

You can spot weld the nickel strips to the BMS or solder it to the PCB pad. I preferred to solder the nickel strips to the PCB for a sturdy connection. First, apply soldering flux to the PCB pads and end of the nickel strips. After that in all the pads by applying a little amount of solder and then solder them together.

Figure a:

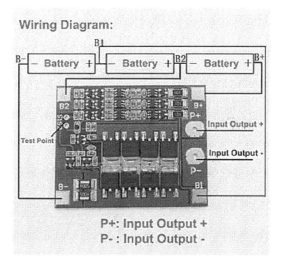

Figure b:

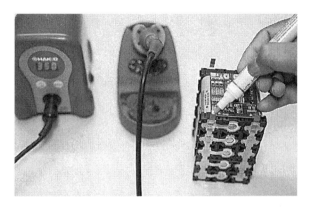

Figure c:

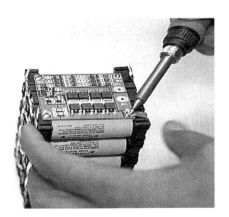

Figure d:

- **Step 10: External non-conductive cover**

Cover the battery pack with an external cover to prevent short circuit as the Ni strips are exposed, the cover should be non-metallic, creating a custom 3D print mount is preferable.

- **Step 11: Wiring the components**

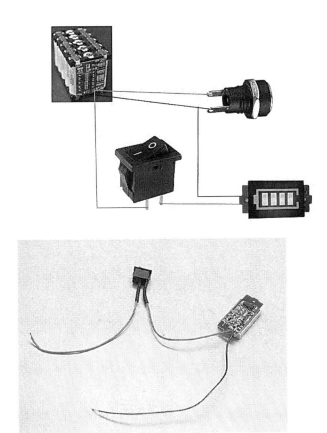

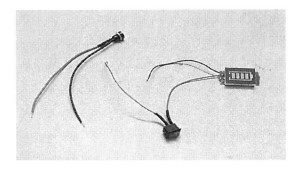

Figure: Wiring

Normally a standard battery has only two terminal for connecting the load and to charge the battery. Apart from this, I have added a battery level indicator, to see the battery level whenever required. I have used a 5mm DC jack (12V /3A) for input/ output, 3S battery level indicator module to see the battery status and a rocker switch to ON/OFF the battery level indicator.

- **Step 12: Final assembling**

First, install the components into the respective slots in the 3D printed enclosure. You can see the above picture.

Solder the positive (red wire) from the DC jack and Rocker switch to the P+ of the BMS, negative wires from the DC jack and Battery level indicator to the P- of BMS.

Then apply hot glue at the base of the battery compartment, then secure the battery pack. So that it will seats firmly and prevent any loosing of wire connections.

Now the battery pack is ready to use.

Chapter 12: Battery Management System (BMS)

Battery management system is a device that guarantees safe and reliable battery operation. To maintain the safety and reliability of the battery, state monitoring and evaluation, charge control, and cell balancing are functionalities that have been implemented in BMS. As an electrochemical product, a battery acts differently under different operational and environmental conditions. The uncertainty of a battery's performance poses a challenge to the implementation of these functions. This chapter addresses concerns for current BMSs. A state evaluation of a battery, including the state of charge, state of health, and state of life, is a critical task for a BMS. Through reviewing the latest methodologies for the state evaluation of batteries, the future challenges for BMSs are presented and possible solutions are proposed as well.

12.1 Battery Cell Balancing

Different algorithms of cell balancing are often discussed when multiple serial cells are used in a battery pack for a particular device. The means used to perform cell balancing typically include bypassing some of the cells during charge (and sometimes during discharge) by connecting external loads parallel to the cells through controlling corresponding FETs. The typical by-pass current ranges from a few milliamps to amperes.

A difference in cell voltages is a most typical manifestation of unbalance, which is attempted to be corrected either instantaneously or gradually through by-passing cells with higher voltage. However, the underlying reasons for voltage differences on the level of battery chemistry and discharge kinetics are not widely understood. Therefore goals and extent of bypassing charge cannot be clearly defined and attempted balancing can often achieve more harm than good. In fact, many common cell balancing

Schemes based on voltage only result in a pack more unbalanced that without them.

12.1.1: Types of Cell Balancing

There are two main methods for battery cell charge balancing: passive and active balancing.

The natural method of passive balancing a string of cells in series can be used for lead-acid, nickel-based batteries and Li-ion Batteries. These types of batteries can be brought into light overcharge conditions without permanent cell damage. When the overcharge is small, the excess energy is released by increasing the cell body temperature. The excess energy can be released by the external circuit connected in parallel to each cell. This circuit consists of a power resistor connected in series with a control MOSFET. This method can be used for all types of batteries but is effective for a small number of cells in series.

The active balancing method is based on the active transport of the energy among the cells. This balancing method does not depend on the chemical characteristics of the cells and can be used for most types of modern batteries. There are several types of active balancing methods based on the type of energy transfer. The energy transfer can be from one cell to the whole battery, from the whole battery to one cell, or from cell to cell. Each energy transfer is based on the type of dedicated DC-to-DC converter. The energy is transferred from the strongest cell to the whole battery or other cells, and from the battery or other cells to the weakest cell.

- **Passive or dissipative Balancing**

In the automotive and transportation marketplace, large battery stacks provide high output power without producing harmful emissions (i.e. carbon monoxide and hydrocarbons) associated with gasoline-powered combustion engines. Ideally, each individual battery in the stack equally contributes to the system. However, when it comes to batteries, all batteries are not created equally. Even batteries of the same chemistry with the same physical size and shape can have different total capacities, different internal resistances, different self-discharge rates, etc. In addition, they can age differently, adding another variable to the battery life equation.

A battery stack is limited in performance by the lowest capacity cell in the stack; once the weakest cell is depleted, the entire stack is effectively depleted. The health of each individual battery cell in the stack is determined based on its state of charge (SoC) measurement, which measures the ratio of its remaining charge to its cell capacity. SoC uses battery measurements such as voltage, integrated charge and discharge currents and temperature to determine the charge remaining in the battery. Precision single-chip and multi-chip battery management systems (BMS) combine battery monitoring (including SoC measurements) with passive or active cell balancing to improve battery stack performance. These measurements result in:

a) Healthy battery state of charge independent of the cell capacity
b) Minimized cell-to-cell state of charge mismatch
c) Minimized effects of cell aging (aging results in lost capacity)

Initially, a battery stack may have fairly matched cells. But over time, the cell matching degrades due to charge/discharge cycles, elevated temperature, and general aging. A weak battery cell will charge and discharge faster than stronger or higher capacity cells and thus it becomes the limiting factor in the run-time of a system. Passive balancing allows the stack to look like every cell has the same capacity as the weakest cell. Using a relatively low current, it drains a small amount of energy from high SoC cells during the charging cycle so that all cells charge to their maximum SoC. This is accomplished by using a switch and bleed resistor in parallel with each battery cell

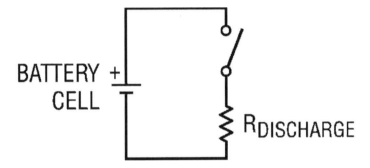

Figure: Passive Cell Balancer with Bleed Resistor

The high SoC cell is bled off (power is dissipated in the resistor) so that charging can continue until all cells are fully charged.

Passive balancing allows all batteries to have the same SoC, but it does NOT improve the run-time of a battery-powered system. It provides a fairly low-cost method for balancing the cells, but it wastes energy in the process due to the discharge resistor. Passive balancing can also correct for the long-term mismatch in self-discharge current from cell to cell.

- ## Active or Non-dissipative balancing

Each type of DC-to-DC converter used has its own characteristics. The final decision depends mainly on the electrical power sourced from the battery, on the battery capacity in ampere-hours (Ah), and on the final application requirements. This example uses a charge transfer between individual cells. The block schematic is shown in Figure.

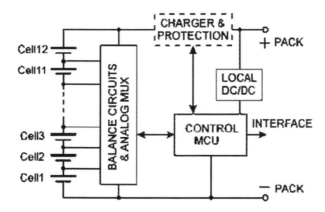

Figure: Block Schematic

The energy transfer is based on the inductive storage element. The energy is accumulated into inductance by the MOSFET switch from the strong cell, and in the next cycle, it is released into the closest weak cell. The amount of the transferred energy in one step depends mainly on the final application—it depends on the discharge current and the required cell-balancing speed. In accordance with these requirements, the inductor, its maximum current, and other circuit element parameters must be selected.

The balancing is active during the charging period, to maintain an equal state of charge (SOC) for each cell at the end of charge. The application is used daily so that different discharges due to the

95

different leakage currents of the cells are not important. The balancing is active in the discharge period too, so this circuit maintains an equal discharge for each cell, both strong and weak. The energy from the strong cells is transferred into the weak cells.

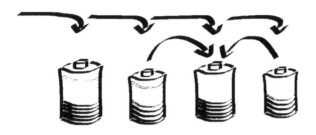

Figure: Basic representation of active balancing

12.2 BMS Technology

BMS devices come in different states in the market based on the application of the user.

Few of the variants of these are Analog BMS devices which are simple and do not have many options whereas Digital BMS is very sophisticated and much more complex in application.

12.3 Topology

BMS topologies fall into 3 categories:

- Centralized: a single controller is connected to the battery cells through a multitude of wires
- Distributed: a BMS board is installed at each cell, with just a single communication cable between the battery and a controller

- Modular: a few controllers, each handing a certain number of cells, with communication between the controllers.

12.4 Choosing a Battery Management System

Based on your application and needs you will have to choose a proper BMS for the safe operation of your battery/battery pack.

For example, you need a BMS for a portable Bluetooth speaker. For this, the basic requirements are under voltage protection, over temperature protection, over current, and overcharge protection.

In this case, you can use many off the shelf BMS IC's which offer most of these basic features. Some also include charging, this means that you need not worry about adding some more electronics for managing a small battery and it could be done with just one small IC and a few supporting electronics.

BMS's are not just limited to the above-mentioned features, some of the most prominent features are battery capacity measurement, state of charge(SOC), state of health(SOH) and balancing which was mentioned in the previous chapters.

If the battery packs are large/ contain a large number of cells/ there are many packs connected together and knowing the status of each cell is critical, in this case, communication between the packs/cells with the main board is important. Usually, there will be a master BMS and many slave BMS connected to it. This may be connected via CAN/UART. These types are currently in use in electric vehicles, large-scale power storage to name a few

Some of these complex BMS's are available commercially where it is sold based on the capacity, features, type of balancing, number of cells it can manage to name a few.

In case of an electric vehicle, you will have a large number of cells to look after. Failure of one cell is a serious issue. Fire in these packs will cause a domino effect and might explode. Hence, we will have to monitor and balance a lot of cells. This will be taken care by a slave BMS on each module, this will look into the actual capacity in the cells, degradation, state of health abnormal heating etc. All the data collected is sent to main or master BMS which estimates the capacity left, the time required for recharge and many other parameters. With these details, you can estimate the range of your vehicle.

Even in your smartphones and laptops, there is a complex BMS which monitors everything. The battery capacity is not estimated in terms of voltage because it varies a lot based on the load. So, what they do is use one of those BMS's mentioned above which will do a few cycles of the cell which will get a reference for the actual capacity of the cell. Once the battery starts draining, the discharge of the cell is monitored. Based on how much of the actual capacity was used you get the battery percentage.

If you are the kind of person who digs deep into your phone's setting you might have come across an option named "reset fuel gauge". This is used to make the BMS take new reference of the battery capacity.

You can go through many electronics suppliers for these different IC's or readymade BMS boards.

This is just a small insight into the world of BMS's and a few common types available in the market now. Do your research before choosing a BMS or else it will be a surprise firework show.

Chapter 13: The Present breakthrough in Battery Technology.

13.1 Solid-state batteries

Though still a nascent technology, solid-state batteries are hot right now. Among the most prominent proponents is Toyota, which aims to commercialize solid-state batteries for electric cars by 2022.

Solid state batteries traditionally offer stability but at the cost of electrolyte transmissions. A paper published by Toyota scientists writes about their tests of a solid-state battery which uses sulfide superionic conductors. All this means a superior battery.

The result is a battery that can operate at super capacitor levels to completely charge or discharge in just seven minutes - making it ideal for cars. Since its solid state that also means it's far more stable and safer than current batteries. The solid-state unit should also be able to work in as low as minus 30 degrees Celsius and up to one hundred.

Other auto competitors are close on Toyota's heels in the rush to satisfy government mandates for emission-free alternatives to gasoline- and diesel-powered vehicles. BMW, for example, has also indicated a keen interest in developing solid-state batteries for their promise of better safety and higher energy density.

13.2 Grabat graphene batteries

The Spanish company Graphenano has introduced a graphene-polymer battery that could allow electric vehicles to have a maximum range of a staggering 800 kilometers. The battery can also be charged in just a few minutes.

The company notes that the battery is designed for a number of uses, and could be put in houses, bicycles, drones, and even pacemakers. Dubbed Grabat, the batteries will be manufactured in Yecla, Spain and will have an energy density of 1,000 Wh/kg (for comparison, lithium batteries generally have an energy density of 180 Wh/kg). Grabat will also have a voltage of 2.3 V.

If that's not enough, the battery could discharge and charge faster than a standard lithium-ion battery (almost 33 times that of lithium). It also does not exhibit a memory effect, a phenomenon in which charging a battery multiple times lowers its maximum energy potential.

Best of all, independent analyses by TÜV and Dekra have demonstrated that the batteries are safe and are not prone to explosions like lithium batteries, and tests conducted by the company have shown that, after being short-circuited, the battery is able to return to work with 60% of the load.

13.3 Prieto Battery innovation: Foam technology

Startup Prieto Battery spun out of Colorado State University, is focused on all the three major components of the existing battery architecture. Their environmentally-friendly, water-based manufacturing process is highly repeatable, easily scalable, and very cost effective. Prieto Battery claims that this ground-up approach redefines the standard for battery production and performance and is necessary to break out of the decades-long incremental approach to building a better battery. The goal - a battery that is safe, has more power, charges faster, lasts longer, costs less and can be used across a variety of applications and devices.

Prieto believes the future of batteries is 3D. The company has managed to crack this with its battery that uses a copper foam substrate.

This means these batteries will not only be safer, thanks to no flammable electrolyte, but they will also offer longer life, faster charging, five times higher density, be cheaper to make and be smaller than current offerings.

Prieto aims to place its batteries into small items first, like wearables. But it says the batteries can be upscaled so we could see them in phones and maybe even cars in the future.

13.4 Ryden dual carbon battery

Power Japan Plus has already announced this new battery technology called Ryden dual carbon. Not only will it last longer and charge faster than lithium but it can be made using the same factories where lithium batteries are built.

The batteries use carbon materials which mean they are more sustainable and environmentally friendly than current alternatives. It also means the batteries will charge twenty times faster than lithium ion. They will also be more durable, with the ability to last up to 3,000 charge cycles, plus they are safer with a lower chance of fire or explosion.

Chapter 14: Potential Hazard

Batteries are self-contained chemical reactors capable of transforming chemical energy into electrical energy on demand. The chemicals used in batteries are corrosive and toxic and may cause personal injuries or equipment damage if they escape from any battery. Most of the batteries available in regular commerce are quite abuse resistant and effectively contain the corrosive and toxic substances under normal user conditions. The escape of the battery contents, if it occurs, is generally caused by inadvertent or deliberate abuse or some form of mishandling. Battery defects introduced by poorly controlled manufacturing operations may also lead to containment problems. The majority of batteries, both rechargeable batteries, and non-rechargeable batteries, are chemically unstable. Slow chemical reactions occur in batteries whether they are in use or not, and energy is released by these reactions. If for any reason batteries are exposed to conditions that accelerate the rate of these reactions to a significant extent, the energy may be released so fast that the batteries rupture or explode. The disposal of batteries in fires or incinerators is certain to cause ruptures or explosions.

- Flammable Gases

Batteries emit flammable hydrogen gas, especially during charge and discharge cycles. Hydrogen ignites easily and can cause a fire or explosion if allowed to accumulate in a small area.

Hydrogen is not toxic, but at high concentrations is a highly explosive gas. The 100% LEL concentration of hydrogen is 4.0% by volume.

At this concentration, all it takes is a source of ignition to cause an explosion. Sparking from a battery terminal as it is connected or disconnected from the charging system is more than adequate as a source of ignition energy.

Adequate ventilation should be in place to disperse fumes given off during charging. Clearly, designate areas as "No Smoking" and eliminate the risk of open flames, sparks, welding and electric arcs. Each cell has its own vent cap, designed to allow gases to escape and keep the electrolyte solution from spilling. Check that vent caps are in place to prevent overflow and spilling of dangerous acid.

Fire protection equipment, such as fire extinguishers, should be stored in an easily accessible location nearby. All qualified workers should know how to operate fire extinguishers.

- Electrical Shock

    Batteries are stored energy devices, meaning no overload protection is available if the battery is connected improperly or short-circuited. Always keep a voltmeter handy to verify correct polarity and expected voltage levels when connecting strings of batteries.

    Exercise caution when working with metallic tools or conductors to prevent short circuits and sparks. Remove rings, watches and loose jewelry when working with batteries. Never lay tools or other metal parts on top of a battery.

- The weight of the Battery

    Cells used in large industrial standby-power applications can weigh anywhere from 20 to 100+ pounds apiece. When combined into large battery banks, weights can exceed thousands of pounds.

Use safe lifting techniques while exercising caution of electric shock as discussed above. Work in teams, always lifting with your legs, and use a forklift or similar device when lifting heavy loads. Do not attempt to stop a battery if it slides out of the equipment.

Reference

www.phys.org

www.brighthubengineering.com

https://en.wikipedia.org

www.grandviewresearch.com

http://pveducation.org

http://www.science.uwaterloo.ca

www.sciencedirect.com

http://www.electric-skateboard.builders

Automotive battery Technology by Alexander Thaler

www.eetimes.com

www.accessengineeringlibrary.com

www.huffingtonpost.com.au

in.reuters.com

cleantechnica.com

www.offgridenergyindependence.com

www.pocket-lint.com

www.sciencedaily.com

www.extremetech.com

futurism.com

Revolution-green.com

cen.acs.org

community.openenergymonitor.org

Isidor Buchmann – Batteries in a portable world

.

Made in the USA
Middletown, DE
06 November 2019

78096864R00062